BONE LOVE

Florida Technological University
Contemporary Poetry Series

Other works in the series:
David Posner, *The Sandpipers*
Edmund Skellings, *Heart Attacks*
Edmund Skellings, *Face Value*

BONE LOVE

by

Malcolm Glass

A Florida Technological University Book

UNIVERSITY PRESSES OF FLORIDA — Orlando

Typographical design and composition by Martin S. Gator
Printed by Storter Printing Company, Gainesville

Library of Congress Cataloging in Publication Data

Glass, Malcolm.
    Bone love.

    (Florida Technological University contemporary
poetry series.
    "A Florida Technological University book."

    I. Title. II. Series: Florida Technological Univer-
sity. F.T.U. contemporary poetry series.
PS 3557.L344B6   1978 811′.5′4 78-14337
ISBN 0-8130-0616-3

Acknowledgments

The author would like to thank the Southern Federation of State Arts Agencies for a Literary Fellowship and the publishers of the poems in this volume that have appeared previously for their permission to reprint them here:

"An Afternoon with Allen Tate" is reprinted by permission from *Green River Review* 1 (Spring 1969). "Traveling" is reprinted by permission of *Florida Quarterly*. "Metro Passengers" is reprinted by permission from *Puddingstone* 2 (Spring 1975). "Sacré Coeur" and "Sailing" are reprinted by permission from *Kansas Quarterly* 4 (Winter 1971–72). "Driving Back to Kentucky" is reprinted by permission from *Mountain Review* (Summer 1975).

"Seeing" was first published in *Sewanee Review* 85 (Summer 1977). Copyright 1977 by the University of the South. Reprinted by permission of the editor. "Drowning" and "Braille" are reprinted by permission from *The New Orleans Review* 5 (3). "Specters" is reprinted by permission from *Arlington Quarterly* 3 (Winter 1970–71). "The Belfry" is reprinted by permission from *The Panhandler* 3 (1977). "Flying North on April Third" is reprinted by permission from *Cimmaron Review* 9 (September 1969), where it appeared under the title "Flying North from Nashville on April 3rd." "Crux" copyright 1971 by Christian Century Foundation. Reprinted by permission from the February 24, 1971, issue of *The Christian Century*.

"Hunting Spiders" is reprinted by permission from *Ball State University Forum* 18 (Autumn 1977). "Trade" is reprinted by permission from *Karamu* 4 (February 1976), where it appeared under the title "Exchange." "The Tricyclist" is reprinted by permission from *FOCUS/Midwest*, vol. 8, no. 54; copyright 1971 by *FOCUS/Midwest* Publishing Co., Inc. "Art" is reprinted by permission from *The Andover Review* 1 (Spring 1974). "Martin Collins" is reprinted by permission from *Southern Poetry Review* 11 (Fall 1970), where it appeared under the title "The Death of Martin Collins."

"At Rock Springs River," "Finding the Way," and "Keeping the Winter" are reprinted by permission from *Vanderbilt Poetry Review*, 2 (1977) and 3 (1978). "Knowing" is reprinted by permission from *Poem* 16 (November 1972), where it appeared under the title "The Stripper." "Bone Love" is reprinted by permission from *Prairie Schooner* (Spring 1974). "Waking" is reprinted by permission from *Mississippi Review* 1 (1972). "She Says" is reprinted by permission from *The Fiddlehead* 85 (May–July 1970), where it appeared under the title "from *Rocks, Like Words*, III."

"Four Glances at a Newsphoto of a Wedding Couple" is reprinted by permission from *Karamu* 3 (October 1972), where it appeared under the title "Four Glances at a Newsphoto of a Couple after Their Wedding." "Miss Oakhurst" is reprinted by permission from *Mississippi Review* 2 (1973). "One Day" is reprinted by permission from *Corduroy* 5 (1973). "Crossing the Bayou de Chien," "Points of View," and "Cold" are reprinted by permission from *Appalachian Journal* 1 (Autumn 1973), where the last of these appeared under the title "In the Motel Lobby." "Church-Stable" is reprinted by permission from *The Small Farm* 4 (October 1976), 5 (March 1977).

For the reader

Contents

I

The Tricyclist

The sidewalk mumbles
to my wheels, cracks
clicking like train rails.

Sandspurs, sprigging
from the grass, chew
at the edges of my tracks.

The world is sunlight
and leaves in a long
swallow of wind,

and my shadow blinks
across the eyes
of ants and crickets.

I stop. My front wheel
touching the garage door.
The wind dies. I hold

my breath
and begin
to disappear.

Magic

I practiced magic in a mirror,
fanning cards in a swirl
of pips, pulling red silk
green. From my fingers
coins rose, straight and
unfaltering as the tug
of thread.
   I worked the
effects, the dumb-fingered
trickery, hinge and swivel
clicking their teeth.
I watched the glass,
trying to see through
my own misdirection.

I tried to be magician, maker,
spectator, fool; but I could
not do it.

   No one ever does.

That was the secret I didn't know.

And still don't quite believe.

Art

Every
day, after
lunch we colored
sailboats and I got a
headache looking at yellow.
The sun stared at me from the end
of my crayon; the boat burned off the
page. One time I tried to turn a yellow
boat blue so it would rise off the lake of white
paper like a kite, but it turned green and became a

tree.

When the teacher put a red X in the square, I decided
to stick to yellow crayons and headaches.

In the Australian Oak

— for my mother

Mid-Atlantic, I climbed
out of my cockpit and shinnied
up the struts to the upper
wing, where I stood on flimsy
fabric, braced by the
thinnest limbs, the topmost
leaves brushing my face.

The wind leaned me out,
over palm trees thirty feet
below, their fronds arcing
in fountains to the grass
swimming away to the house,
to the kitchen window
where my mother stood
peeling carrots.

I did not believe falling
was possible, yet she
knew . . . and still let me
ride the dare. She held
me safe across the ocean
and the ice wind.

Martin Collins

When Martin Collins died, I remembered
him at slaughtering: how he eased
the hog down the mouth of the oil drum
into the scalding water, and scraped
the hide, his knife blade shivering
down the skin; how he hung him
by his hamstrings from a tree and split
the tension of the flesh to let
the entrails fall in a splattering
of blood over the brim of his hands.

And I remembered dreaming of him
riding in that carcass, huddled
dying in the hog's boned hull,
floating like moonlight on a lake,
a shoreless hero adrift.

He has left me only death.
And I cling to it as if it were my own.

At Rock Springs River,

I swung out on the rope
tied in the cypress, my
bones heavy for that water,
clear as the eyes of sleep,
sliding into the downswing,
my feet skimming the surface,
then climbing, blood pulling
against muscle, lifting me
to the point just before
the line of my arc turned
inside-out; and at that
moment, I dropped, solid
and straight as a watermelon,
broke the barrier, and sank
into the other side of gravity:

      Marbled sunlight
      rippled across
      white sand. Bream
      darted, like sparrows,
      into the cover of
      leaves.
           Above me,
      a new sky wavered,
      warping everything
      but color.
              I could
      see that nothing

under that sky ever
died, free from
breathing; but I
could not stay
down in that heavy
corridor. I tried.
(Sit cross-legged
in this garden. Sit
down.)
       But I rose,
like a rice-paper
balloon, falling
into the sun, until
I broke through

to the raw air screaming down.

Knowing

I sneaked into a carnival show
the summer I turned fifteen
to know woman at last, to see her
clearer than I had ever dreamed.

The lights dimmed. A saxophone
bray and grinding beat shattered
the loudspeakers. A spotlight.
And the star hunched onstage.

She worked her way down to a whirl
of tassels and a G-string sequined
with quivering light—the only
mask between me and the final truth.

As the last chord spilled over her body
she flashed—then ground down slow
to peel. The spotlight tightened in
as she bumped and snapped her way off stage.

Even then I knew I had seen
nothing I did not already know.
I understood everything she had
to say. Her need to tell me nothing.

The Green Coat

— for Ann and Jerry Girardeau

Jerry's green coat rides me
too large, empty
on my shoulders. The sleeves
swallow my arms.

> Sunday afternoons he was
> magic—green and quick:
> At his fingertips, cards
> turned to light, were
> light, were gone. He
> stuffed his cigarette
> into a fresh handkerchief,
> the ember eating
> the center, then shook
> the cloth out—all char and ash
> vanished—a white square,
> perfect.
>   But the best
> trick was the dime
> gone in a snap
> of finger on thumb.

My mother says,
"Have it taken up. Go to a
good tailor.
He'll make it fit right."

I snap a dime up my sleeve.

II

Bone Love

— for Anne

Ankle bones, elbows,
and knees. The corners
of your geography.

I never think of
loving these rocks
and hard places,

mapping the angular
edges of your body,
never think to polish

these stones with the
palm of my hand. Perhaps
I do not want you

solid, cool as bone:
Your skeleton rises
to meet me. And ankle

bones elbows and knees
pull me inland
to the sea.

Waking

The chatter of birds splashed the sky.
I woke. Then ebbed away
again on the thin tide of sleep.

Waking should be tried and final
like steel, swift as sparrows
breaking a border of trees.

But that morning I drowned
over and over, remembering
when you dreamed of me in her arms
and woke to cry alone, afraid to wake me.

Snaky Lady

She put her fingers in
my mouth while the snake
between her legs started
sliding around my waist,
climbing my body
breathless, bristling
the hair on my chest.

I clenched my eyes,
staring at the suns dancing
across my skull; I held
on, speechless, my mouth
swollen with fingers,
nails like razors.
                    I only
want, she says, I only want
to love you.

Go Go Girl

Hey

you mothers
out there

you've got me
where I want you

look me
in the eye

if you can

She Says

        to him, shaking out the blanket,
she says, "Candy just weren't no lady,
Bobby, I'm telling you what's right.
No lady does what she done, not even
by mistake. Don't you pull that stuff
on me, you hear? "

        Bobby goes down
to the shore, picks up a flat stone
and skims it out over the lake:
one   two   threefour
skips rippling the water in rings—
an ellipsis in the afternoon.

Four Glances at a Newsphoto of a Wedding Couple

1. *Bliss*
They smile
white as candles,
just one moment
before the altar rail
wraps around their knees
and the flowers burst into flame.

2. *She*
Her veil is a cake
so light it could
fly swifter
than tufted
titmice.

3. *He*
The ink of his trousers
weighs him into the carpet
and he clutches
at the hem of his white
jacket to hold his chin
above the sea of ferns,
to hold his eyes above
his drowning smile.

4. *Joined*

The ribbons spill from her bouquet
like three knotty convent vows.
She dreams no more of falling
from fire escapes. She has wed
a heavenly kingdom of blood
no god would think
to put asunder.

Miss Oakhurst

On June fourteenth Miss Oakhurst turned
thirty-three, and the library staff greeted her
thirtieth birthday over coffee and cake again,
never speaking of marriage or her single

solitude, of course. On the first of July her
European tour began: the Mediterranean again.
In a flurry of bright postcards (not a single
day missed) her news came back. Each one in turn

we tacked on the bulletin board. And again
in August she returned—reticent and single,
but no longer prim. She had overturned
decorum in a single revolution and round trip: her

hemlines raised above the knee, her single
ring now three, her lashes darkened, turned
up against pale-blue eye shadow, her
slender legs haze-gray in textured hose. Again,

no one spoke of singularity, but we knew the turn
and change she had breathed, still glowing on her
skin. And knew she would not change again.
Somewhere in Athens, Rome or Florence a single

sunrise broke midsummer and let her
eyes see all her loveliness in fire again.
And then she walked in haze and smoke, a single
flame dancing simple lines and turns

behind a subtle veil.
                    October has come again.
Miss Oakhurst follows the revolution of each single
day through proper channels: books returned,
overdue, discharged. Upstairs in the stacks her

book cart whispers down the carpet through single
aisles that wall her in with bookspines. Turning
at the window she sees the reflection of her
eyes against the autumn sky. Downstairs again:

Discharge. Return. Reshelve. Return.
Her chain of being.   And over Rome
the single sun breaks the sky again and again.

One Day

it was
night for a week
like a heart
murmur
of the sun

her hand
on the drowning match

salt on my
lips and teeth

One week we did
not breathe
to keep the sun
crushed
between our
hip bones

No One

I slide my fingers
into your extravagant
black hair, tunneling
through blind. Your
head shapes my palms—
hidden, secret—
my fingertips only
dreaming skin.

No one will ever
hold you so gently.

Not even death

III

Crossing the Bayou de Chien

The water lay sleeping
like a full moon, still
reaching into the clay
for bones lying tens
of thousands of years below.

For a moment I heard
the cries of dogs
drowning.

Church-Stable

Hay stacked along the walls,
spilling out of the corners
into the middle of the floor.
Straw and dung where blacked
shoes scuffed at varnish.

Windows up or knocked out,
toothless and gawking. Listen
to the rumble of counterweights
in the walls, to the kerosene
stove cracking its knuckles.

The pulpit lies down speechless.
The ceiling rises to the gable—
tongue-and-groove oak paneling
in God-sized herring-bone.
This ark, this ship of cattle.

Capsized. Up-side-down in a field.

Points of View

From a massive bald of rock
jutting over the thick ravine,
I watched hawks planing over treetops
below. Slowing in the up-wind
buffets, they came about and stretched
the curl of the turn into a down-wind run.

I could see new shades of gray
flared in their wings,
the curve of upper camber,
the dihedral lifting bone
from the narrow bridge
between their shoulders,
their beaks threading the wind.

They seemed to lie sleeping
on the rim of a thermal sea,
but in my veins I knew their secret,
the taut patience
tugging them
earthward.

Swinging Bridge on Kentucky 421

The boy crosses over
the stream from house to
roadside, walking the mist
on gray boards laid across
two cables, the bridge rising
and falling under his steps.

He stands at the roadside
waiting for the schoolbus,
one foot on the guardrail,
his fatigue cap pulled down,
and stares over the stream
into the hazy sunlight
slanting down the gray brown
hillside through bare trees.

After school, he crosses back,
bouncing, making the boards
talk to each other, like
starlings' wings.
                    He knows
his way so well he could go
sleepwalking or blind,
the stream unbroken, the ground
buried under water—over and back,
and back, and back

Cold

The old farmer,
retired to the hotel,
sits in the lobby

on warm January days
praying for zero
weather. "This is

what makes a man sick,"
he says, "all this
changing from cold

to hot, and back,
like a fever. I like
winter when it means

to keep cold."
He closes his eyes:
a pond in a blaze

of ice and sunlight,
cattle melting the air
with their breath.

"Get cold," he says.
"Stay cold."

An Afternoon with Allen Tate

The sun slants down the Cumberland, and pulls
the edge of shadows down the faded wall
past china press and sagging bookshelves. Across
the mirror and the candelabra falls

a static haze. Dim sunlight raises dust
like ghosts of slower time: forgotten skills
and graces, dress more elegant. The sword
hanging above the hearth shall be used to kill

no more. Retained for emblematic strength,
it guards the honor of a lost duress.
Among these remnants of a history
we have not lived, we pay our homage, bless

the past by coming here before this slender
man to listen to his words relive
tradition. But our colloquy is safe.
At first our talk is sheltered, tentative;

then we shift to guarded, academic ground,
and finally fall to turning over names
like leafing through the index of a book:
"Andrew was too ill to come; he blames

old age. Red looked a little thin last fall.
And Don retires this year. I heard that they
have planned another book on us, reprinting
all the early poems. I had prayed

that my apprentice work would be forgotten,
or suppressed."
                    But he should know the past
won't give him up. Those years, like a triskelion,
track him down, and every mirror casts

reflections of a tall-skulled Lazarus
in ashy flesh. Yet in his dying, his head
held steady, true, he is a god-like man—
too certain of his time to betray the dead.

Traveling

Two hitchhikers:
an old man in an overcoat
down to his ankles, a battered
pasteboard box
at his feet,
and five miles later
a college boy in a blazer and tie
with his steel-gray aluminum suitcase
and paper sign.

I would have picked them up, but they were going
the wrong way. And the signs said, "Keep Off Median"
to tell me I should know where I'm going.

I flashed by them, hunched under the wheel
in my metal shell, skinning the living
daylights out of time.

Two men still as trees.
                              And I—white steel
chrome and glass streaking the highway
like a splash of sunlight.

A bleached pasteboard box
full of dusty bones, an empty
suitcase with blood stains
in the lining, the late sun scattering
gravel and clay down the shoulder of the road.

Metro Passengers

The doors wheeze, slam shut,
and the latch clatters locked.
The crowded car lurches away
against a sliding collage of posters.

We ride staring nowhere,
until the old woman gets on.
She sits at the front of the car
on a pull-down seat, facing us.

Holding her head lifted
as though she were listening
for a forgotten song,
she weeps silently,
her face shining,
an open mirror.

We stare in every direction
but hers. And finally
our faces turn her away
toward the window

Sacré Coeur

— from "Baedeker Prudhomme"

You won't fail to see it—not likely. From any
high place in the city—an étage
of the rattling maze of the Eiffel Tower, or from
the sooty parapets of gargoyled

Notre Dame—look north-north-east
of the Ile. If you are lucky (and many
tourists are) the sun will be out
and the church will seem to be rising from

the French soil, hovering above its hill
(always above the city), glowing at the least
(sometimes shimmering) in the sun, like
a mid-day moon, through the smog. No doubt

it is impressive, hanging there. But
up close (and to get there you have one hell
of a climb from the metro stop), Sacré Coeur
is altogether obvious. It may strike

you (as it did me) that the building, as such,
is obscenely bald, a naked exhibition, yet
unashamed for all that, like a bastard
orphan, blissful in ignorance, her

naïveté her only grace. But on
the other hand, she comprehends too much
architecture: Romanesque-Byzantine-
Victorian—the final eclectic word

in styles. The domes on domes, too numerous
to enumerate, ridged as though they were spun
in a potter's atelier, to a columned, domed,
crossed point (it really has to be seen

to seem even falsely real), and rising up,
stage center, the square, innocuous
minaret-campanile, hidden
(down-staged, so to speak) by the central dome.

Taken as a whole, it is a blatant, coy
platitude; a turgid, sentimental
paean—monotonously incremental;
a *tour de force;* an architectural toy.

Cemetery for Children Who Died in the Smallpox Epidemic, 1854

Tawny weeds nod in the dry wind
like mantises; leather ribbons
of gumtree bark lace the yellow
grass and coil around tumbled
headstones like dozing snakes.

In the mesmeric hum of late summer
flies, the children dream they are
koalas chewing pale green gum leaves,
wallabies listening to the mist
of fur in their ears, or emus striding
across lake beds of sand and salt,
the wind parting their feathers
in a straight path down their backs.

And I walk among the gravestones,
dreaming for these children, my body
feverish even in this patch of shade.

Castlemaine, Victoria

Driving Back to Kentucky

A colt rolls on his back,
his mane a small white wave
breaking over his shoulder.
Beyond him in the wind-ruffled
pasture five horses swirl away
from the fence. The hills
drown in the bright shallow
water of the sun.

I try to imagine this
ocean floor after
the fires, after the winds
have licked our bones.

IV

Finding the Way

— for Virgil Cook

1.
With his white cane
scanning the sidewalk
he glides between the trees,

tuning in the scratch
of concrete, the chatter
of leaves, the stuttering

grass.
　　　I sit at my desk
in the library, listening
to the late afternoon traffic

below. I stare over
the top of a redbud tree,
my fingers resting on

page 247, as though the words
were really there.

2.
Taking notes in class,
he stops punching the page

and looks at his watch
with his fingertip:

and I wonder if he ever
pauses long enough to see

the pulse bright under his thumb.

3.
At the party
he stands alone
in the middle

of the crowded room,
listening for someone
to draw him in.

I sit across the
room, paralyzed,
unable to look

at him. He turns
his head and lifts
his palms

to the edges of our
voices, waiting for
one of us to go

blind.

Keeping the Winter

The gray sky fell in a thin snow, sliding
down a tense wind. I hacked at a cedar
for Christmas, cold green tinged with rust,
to keep winter out of the house. I pulled it
to the ground, brushing the bristling
needles from my face like waving away
a nagging swarm of summer gnats.

On the way back I found the carcass
of a dog, frozen fur to bone, hungry
for decay, steam in his belly turning
to ice, his ears listening for green-flies,
his legs stretched in mid-stride.

When the first rain sends the fire
into his coat, he will wake, his stomach
rumbling with the pangs of worms;
his muscles will relax
from the bone, the joints loosening
into the reach of his gait.
The sky will rise, pulling against
the roots of the trees, his fur will
bristle in the mouth of the wind,
and the sun will catch light
in the rain glazing his eyes,
like the promise he kept all winter.

Pappy

1.
That cloudless afternoon
the sun struck the sky
white. His bureau drawer
stood open like the mouth
of a howling fox.
                    The single
pistol shot leapt like lightning
down his spine.
                    On the driveway,
his son's blood lay shallow,
like late afternoon sun
staining a river.

It was an accident. They
kept telling him. It was
an accident.

2.
After that day
he began to live
for sundown, sleeping
on the porch all day,
working while everyone else
slept, tending rows of shrubs
and trees in the nursery, making
rain in the greenhouse, his shadow
sliding along the glass walls
as he moved among the orchids
and bromeliads—his only sunlight
in their leaves.

3.

Years later, angina nagged
his heart, the fiery roots
of pain darting across his
chest and down his arms.

Then cancer, like black
widows drinking the marrow
from his bones.

4.

In a clean bed, the sheets
tight across his body,
he lay staring at the sun
burning through
the night sky.

Drowning

After an evening rain the frogs move in
to cover the bottom land behind the city
dump. Their croaking swells like a moonless
tide washing over the haze.

I slip on my sneakers, load the wheelbarrow
and whisper down the back street past
tin cans, plastic bags, and milk cartons,
past flames coiling in bedsprings,
my shadow stuttering across mountains
of magazines and books.

The frogs have taken the wet grass
for miles around, and they hold
the land with screams, their rasping voices
building layer on layer of hysteria.

I unload the mower, coil the rope
and crank up in a burst of blue flame.
I rev up, drowning the frogs
with my own scream. And then I move in.
I see nothing. I never feel a leg or body
under my shoe. I hear nothing but the mower.

Specters

Out walking in the cedar woods
I saw the bone-stiff carcass of a bird
hanging from a branch
by a kite-string tied at the claw,
  like the rector's son they found last week,
  hanging in the graveyard,
  his flesh chiseled with a score of cigarette burns,
  cross-hatched with a razor.

The bird revolved slowly, a plumb bob
twisting the truth of absolute gravity
out of the raveling plumb line,
his beak drilling the air,

describing the zero only man can comprehend.

Seeing

The first day on the job, he was carrying
a bucket of boiling tar across the roof
we were building, his sneakers sticking
to the black tar paper, leaning like a
diver one hundred feet down dreamwalking
the crush of water, his lead shoes
churning shadows of white sand; and
at that space between the boards
no one could see beneath the paper,
his foot broke through to daylight
below, and he fell forward,
the tar spilling before him, as though
the ground flowed away, thick lava swelling
toward the eaves, blue with the sky in its
mirror shine; and he sprawled face down
and saw, for one moment, black.

And then he saw what he had never seen and
never should have for another sixty years:

Coronas like the pealing of steeple bells
spinning leaves in red halos.

                        His eyes
saw visions prophesying the past in
flaming ladders and fire-wheels
under a sky of Antarctic ice.

And when his eyelids were gone,
seared off quick as steam, he saw
his mother, bright silver lips to colors
melting, stars circling her in a crown
of bells, sleepwalking in a cyclone
of white flame,

and his father, his eyes
blue as veins, drifting across the floor
of an underground sea like a coral fan
uprooted, icy salt sifting through
its bones.

He saw coronas, visions,
the true sun, all that had been, all
that would be, all that was.

Mowing

A blue cloud holds the yard like fog
at four a. m., as the blade whirls in a blur
of steel. Dandelion blooms skim the lawn
like flat stones skipping a stream; wild
onions spray the air with a quick
metallic taste; grasshoppers dive
away from my path.
                         My brain grows light
as wavering gasoline fumes, my only
balance in the handle, cool slick chrome
holding my palms.
                         With my eyes locked in
on the hedge one way, the house coming back,
I walk blind, letting the mower tow me
into numbness.
                         Decibels break across
the threshold of my inner ear, like steam
rushing through my blood, like the vibrations
of a razor blade making its way across a scream.

The Well of the Sky

1.
At dusk his hair brushes his forehead
And at other times
The dark birds dream of him,
measuring branches, their dusty wings crackling

2.
Bronze light combs the grass where he plays
with his cars and motorcycles
on the clay mountain roads
around tree roots

The car in the steep drive
leans against the brake, the knots in the axle creaking
The tread turns its pale imprint on the concrete,
a sigh on rain

He runs to rescue a transfer truck
about to be flattened by a snowtire
He reaches up
and pushes against cold steel
He stands, turns to run back
to the edge of the driveway, to the end of the bumper
He leans against the chrome, takes another step before
his knee buckles and he falls, rolling over
to see the dark birds, the branch
rising

The Belfry

A narrow oak door
stood propped in the corner
of the choir loft,
and behind it, a dark
spiral of stairs.
I climbed like a diver

going up for air,
and pushed back
the heavy trap door
to surface into light.
Fine-mesh screen
surrounded me. Above,

bell and spire marked
the noon of silence.
And on the floor,
shrouded by spider webs
and soot, lay four
dead pigeons.

V

Braille

My fingers trail across the page
like a witch doctor reading
toad skins. I listen to this

colorless ink, but cannot tell
an *M* from a *6*. Dots cluster
and blur into the whorls

of my fingertips. I close
my eyes tightly and read
heat lightning on my

eyelids. No one can tell me
what I should see; I
don't even know

what I cannot see.
My fingers go numb.
And then I understand.

My hands are blind, dead.
Dumbly, they translate
the code to a curse:

Leper! Leper!

Flying North on April Third

— for Martin Luther King, Jr.

The earth is scarred with lakes
and the cuts of rivers; the hills
and ridges fan out in brittle
star-fingers, like frost
crystalled on a window.

A car skims on rain
to the next crossroads.
Fire hums along high
tension lines. And somewhere
a man cleans his rifle patiently.

But at twenty-nine thousand feet,
I do not even think of praying.

Crux

Job spat,
leaned on the other
buttock, shifting
boils. He abandoned
dreams of gopher wood
and trapped rams, and
prepared himself, by denial
of the hammer of his blood
against the tide of pus,
for the simple martyrdom
of desertion to God.

Job spat out
the bitter phlegm of visions
and theologies, the acid taste
of self-righteousness.

His body had sustained him
beyond the counsel
of the body
                    at last

Hunting Spiders

— for Oather Van Hyning

Under a moon turning
September, I walked the dirt road
with Howard and his father,
following the bank of the river
under a meteor shower, stars
falling out of August.

Pappy said he'd teach us
how to hunt for spiders.
We laughed.

But he strapped a miner's light
to his head and in seconds
called out that he had sighted
the first spider.

With the lamp in the center
of my forehead, I scanned
the roadside weeds, the beam
staring always where I looked.
And Pappy was right. The light
struck two drops of mercury—
the eyes of a spider.
                    Homing in
down the channel of light, I found
him on his web, paralyzed
by my third eye, moon
and stars held still.

Ice

— for my father

On the way home that night, we
drove from central Florida
to the Bering Strait: thin snow
sifting through palm fronds
and pine needles, sleet bouncing,
singing off our windshield.
I listened. The way my father
always listened to me
those flat miles of scrub
to school and back every day.

Some sounds are once
only. This one time,
I said nothing.
And my father, listening,
drove the long way home,
through orange groves
and Australian oaks,
until the arctic
left us behind.

And now, half my life
later, after the first
ice storm of the year,
I find these oak leaves,
half an inch thick
with ice, like marble
polished by slow rains,
like words I cannot
remember, words I don't need
to remember.

Third Grade

One day she told
us to write
a poem. I knew

what that was.
Four lines. Rhymes.
A title. About

something poems
are about. I could
see it in print

on a page. My
poem. All I had to
do was copy it down.

But I couldn't see
the words. The page
shrank. My hands

froze. My eyes
were fading
to clear blindness.

 I never got a word
on paper. Not even
a title. And it took

me twenty years
to learn the color
of my eyes again.

Trade

I read you poems about dead birds:
pigeons trapped in a belfry; a dove
inside the fence at Westminster,
his wings folded over his dying,
still as summer sun on grass;
a sparrow hanging by a kitestring
from a tree, in a travesty of flight.

And in return, you told me of the morning
you found the dog hanging from the trestle
across from school; and in the courtyard
you showed me the carcass of a bird
fallen from its nest in the eaves.

We traded deaths like marbles,
stuffed our pockets and sleeves with
words, like magicians. At the bell
we said goodbye, laughing, wordless,
and breathing deeply.

Sailing

— for Carlos

Land-loosed, we ghost down harbor,
the sun spraying on the wind-wave
mist. We run the harbor arm
and head up into a dance
of waves slapping counterpoint
to the crackling wake.

The hull strains, heeling,
and the boom dips to pare the waves,
and we, feet locked under the hiking-straps,
lean high to knife the keel
into the chill stone of deep water.

The sail, in foil-curve, wings down
from the masthead, tightening
the shroud to a higher drone.
The sailor's wind-sock—
a plume of red yarn taped
to the shroud—rides the wind
in lazy waves like a feathery
flute solo.

        And our eyes,
sighting past the tip of the mast,
scan the sky. But only for a moment:
Trim the jib, head up a bit tighter,
lean the hull down into plane.

Between the sky and the tension
of canvas, halyards, and spars
is that perfect balance we all
search for—Mozart, Myron, Frost,
you and I—the seabound, the earthbound.

Sleepwalking

—for Dave Till

Step through this window
clean as a needle's
eye and down to the porch
roof suddenly snow suddenly
clay and out onto grass
swimming away pushing
cattails aside and climbing
to the highway breathing
summer
           follow the
stiff yellow line bending
the road to its shoulder
like a man on purpose: gone
to buy soap / gone to deliver
parcels
           walk the patch
of desert at the crossroads
and down the gutted boards
of the old pier where
three boys are fishing
for small sharks / twenty-one
sands and a single hammerhead
the count at noon
                         keep
walking / where you can
this chance you have